Bock's Best

Note: Those titles marked (*) are **brand new arrangements** and do not appear in any other Fred Bock piano collection.

BEFORE YOU GO *FORWARD*, READ THIS *FOREWORD* . . .

There's the King James Version, and now the *New* King James Version, the Living Bible, the Revised Standard Version, the New International Version, the Jerusalem Bible, the New English Bible, even a Cotton-Patch Version. So I'm planning my own version, the CMV: the Church Musicians' Version. My interest here is to "update" Psalm 148 to read: "Sing out (a collective word which I take to mean play as well as sing) your praises with timbrel, and harp, and voices, and organ, *AND PIANO.* "Since the piano, as we know it, was invented by Bartolommeo Cristofori back in 1709, it's clear to me that the Lord was not thinking ahead to the 1980's when pianos would be so pupular in church. Now I can't really blame Him or David, I mean, after all, if the Psalm would have included the word "piano" when it was written, noone would have known what they were talking about, right? In this case, as your CMV paraphraser, I think it is safe to say that the *intent* of that passage was that we use everything at our command to praise God. To some this might be difficult to handle, especially when it includes instruments that plug into the wall like guitars and synthesizers and electric keyboards. Now I'm not claiming Divine Revelation for this paraphrase of Psalm 148, only using it to say that I think we as pianists have a valid expression of our faith through our piano playing as we dedicate our talent to His glory. A piano solo, well-rehearsed and expressively played, can communicate God's message very strongly. I've seen it happen in churches all over the country. God does bless our musical offerings, so it's true, we can praise Him with cymbals, timbrel, organ, *AND PIANO!*

BOCK'S BEST contains fifty piano solo selections I have arranged over the last fifteen years or so. What I did was to go through the list of tunes I've arranged and pick out the ones I felt best about, today, in 1980. There's a wide variety of styles and tunes and treatments. Those of you who know of my work will quickly recognize that this is something I've preached for a long time. Don't get caught up in only one style of playing, or one kind of hymn or gospel song. It takes variety and the ability to adapt to different musical demands to make a good communicator at the 88's.

Back in 1964 (when I was 13!), I issued a collection of piano solos called *The Best of Fred Bock,* published by Word, Inc. It is s[ ] available, and I recommend it to you. There is no duplication [ ] titles between that book and this new book. In fact, BOCK'S BE[ ] contains seven titles which have never appeared in any piano book[ ] mine, ever: BECAUSE HE LIVES; MY TRIBUTE; SWEET, SWE[ ] SPIRIT; THOU ART WORTHY; O HOW HE LOVES YOU A[ ] ME; I AM LOVES; and HE'S EVERYTHING TO ME. These are [ ] very latest arrangements.

Some of you tell me to write my arrangements harder, wh[ ] others tell me to keep it simple. To tell you the truth, when I play[ ] lot and practice like I'm supposed to, the arrangements seem [ ] come out more difficult. If I don't practice, they seem to come o[ ] easier! I suppose that if I practiced every day, I'd probably [ ] writing 32nd notes and glissandos in both hands and in the keys [ ] E, B, and F#. Some of you will undoubtedly start praying that [ ] stop playing altogether!

Now I'd love to sit around and share with you about my pia[ ] arrangements all day, but I've got to get back to my paraphrasi[ ] work. Matthew 24:31 in the CMV says, "And I will send forth ange[ ] with the sound of a mighty *PIANO* to gather the chosen ones fro[ ] the ends of heaven and earth!"

I think this might be the start of something really big!

Sincerely,

Fred

FRED BOCK
June 24, 1980
Los Angeles, California

COMPLETE LISTING OF FRED BOCK PIANO ARRANGEMENTS

PUBLISHER DIRECTORY

1. **ALL-STAR PIANO COLLECTION**, Word, Inc., P.O. Box 1790, Waco, TX 76703
2. **ALLELUIA!** Benson Publishing Company, 365 Great Circle Rd., Nashville, TN 37228
3. **ANGELS, LAMBS, LADYBUGS & FIREFLIES for E-Z Piano/Organ**, Fred Bock Music Company, Alexandria House, Box 300, Alexandria, IN 46001
4. **CRUSADE FAVORITES FROM AROUND THE WORLD**, Word, Inc., P.O. Box 1790, Waco, TX 76703
5. **GOSPEL SONGS FOR PIANO**, Word, Inc., P.O. Box 1790, Waco, TX 76703
6. **GOSPEL SONGS OF STUART HAMBLEN**, Hamblen Music Company, Alexandria House, Box 300, Alexandria, IN 46001
7. **HE TOUCHED ME Piano Book**, Gaither Music Company, Alexandria House, Box 300, Alexandria, IN 46001
8. **HE TOUCHED ME and Other Gaither Favorites for E-Z Piano/Organ**, Gaither Music Company, Alexandria House, Box 300, Alexandria, IN 46001
9. **HOW GREAT THOU ART Piano Book**, Fred Bock Music Company, Alexandria House, Box 300, Alexandria, IN 46001
10. **HYMNTIME PIANO BOOK (Book 1)**, Singspiration, Zondervan Publishing House, 1415 Lake Drive, S.E., Grand Rapids, MI 49506
11. **HYMNTIME PIANO BOOK (Book 2)**, Singspiration, Zondervan Publishing House, 1415 Lake Drive, S.E., Grand Rapids, MI 49506
12. **HYMNTIME PIANO BOOK (Book 3)**, Singspiration, Zondervan Publishing House, 1415 Lake Drive, S.E., Grand Rapids, MI 49506
13. **HYMNTIME PIANO BOOK (Book 4)**, Singspiration, Zondervan Publishing House, 1415 Lake Drive, S.E., Grand Rapids, MI 49506
14. **LATEST HOT FOURTEEN**, Charles Hansen Publications, 1842 West Avenue, Miami Beach, FL 33139
15. **THE Fred Bock LERNER & LOEWE PIANO BOOK**, Chappell Music, Theodore Presser Company, Bryn Mawr, PA 19010
16. **LET'S JUST PRAISE THE LORD Piano Book**, Gaither Music Company, Alexandria House, Box 300, Alexandria, IN 46001
17. **MORE GOSPEL SONGS FOR PIANO**, Word, Inc., P.O. Box 1790, Waco, TX 76703
18. **MY CHRISTMAS PIANO BOOK**, Singspiration, Zondervan Publishing House, 1415 Lake Drive, S.E., Grand Rapids, MI 49506
19. **PIANO SOLOS**, Singspiration, Zondervan Publishing House, 1415 Lake Drive, S.E., Grand Rapids, MI 49506
20. **SACRED SONGS FOR THE PIANO**, Broadman Press, 127 Ninth Ave., N., Nashville, TN 37203
21. **SONGS I SING IN SUNDAY SCHOOL**, Theodore Presser Company, Bryn Mawr, PA 19010
22. **THE BIG NOTE SUNDAY SCHOOL SONGBOOK**, Fred Bock Music Company, Alexandria House, Box 300, Alexandria, IN 46001
23. **SUNDAY SCHOOL SONGS TO SING AND PLAY**, Theodore Presser Company, Bryn Mawr, PA 19010
24. **THE BEST OF FRED BOCK**, Word, Inc., P.O. Box 1790, Waco, TX 76703
25. **THE HIDING PLACE Piano Book**, Fred Bock Music Company, Alexandria House, Box 300, Alexandria, IN 46001
26. **THE KING IS COMING Piano Book**, Benson Publishing Company, 365 Great Circle Rd., Nashville, TN 37228
27. **THE KING IS COMING and OTHER Gaither Favorites for E-Z Piano/Organ**, Gaither Music Company, Alexandria House, Box 300, Alexandria, IN 46001
28. **THE SAVIOR IS WAITING Piano Book**, Fred Bock Music Company, Alexandria House, Box 300, Alexandria, IN 46001
29. **THREE MOODS FOR PIANO**, Gentry Publications, Hinshaw Music, Inc., Box 470, Chapel Hill, NC 27514
30. **YOUNG WORLD PIANIST**, Lillenas Publishing Company, P.O. Box 527, Kansas City, MO 64141
31. **BOCK'S BEST**, Fred Bock Music Company, Alexandria House, Box 300, Alexandria, IN 46001

HE'S EVERYTHING TO ME

RALPH CARMICHAEL
Arranged by Fred Bock

BECAUSE HE LIVES

WILLIAM J. GAITHER
Arranged by Fred Bock

Tenderly, with great feeling and warmth

THOU ART WORTHY

PAULINE MICHAEL MILLS
Arranged by Fred Bock

I AM LOVED

WILLIAM J. GAITHER
Arranged by Fred Bock

Gently

13

SWEET, SWEET SPIRIT

DORIS AKERS
Arranged by Fred Bock

Meditatively

poco a poco accelerando

f

l.h.   *r.h.*

O HOW HE LOVES YOU AND ME

KURT KAISER
Arranged by Fred Bock

MY TRIBUTE

ANDRAÉ CROUCH
Arranged by Fred Bock

Moderato, not too fast

JESUS LOVES ME

(Based on Clair de Lune)

WILLIAM BRADBURY
CLAUDE DEBUSSY
Arranged by Fred Bock

Expressively

24

mf

a little faster

mf

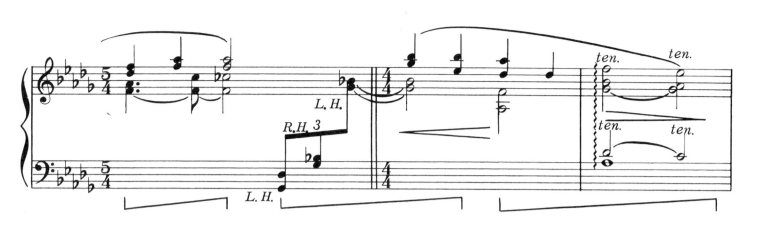

crescendo and accelerando

Slower

IN TIMES LIKE THESE

RUTH CAYE JONES
Arranged by Fred Bock

I JUST FEEL LIKE
SOMETHING GOOD IS ABOUT TO HAPPEN

Words and Music by
WILLIAM J. GAITHER

Bright and happy

HE LIFTED ME

CHARLES H. GABRIEL
Arranged by Fred Bock

GREAT IS THY FAITHFULNESS

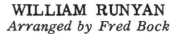

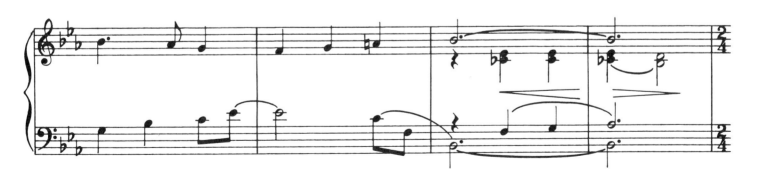

WONDROUS LOVE

American Folk Song
Arranged by Fred Bock

Moderato

TEN THOUSAND ANGELS

RAY OVERHOLT
Arranged by Fred Bock

D. C. al Fine

THE BELL CAROL

M. LEONTOVICH
Arranged by Fred Bock

Sparkling and very rapid

THE CHURCH TRIUMPHANT

Words and Music by
WILLIAM J. and GLORIA GAITHER
Arranged by Fred Bock

I'LL TELL THE WORLD

BAYNARD FOX
Arranged by Fred Bock

8va------

(Melody optional 8va higher)

JESUS IS COMING AGAIN

JOHN W. PETERSON
Arranged by Fred Bock

SOMETHING BEAUTIFUL

Words and Music by
GLORIA and WILLIAM J. GAITHER
Arranged by Fred Bock

THE CHRIST OF EVERY CRISIS

LEE FISHER
Arranged by Fred Bock

In a gentle style

Freely

TEACH ME, LORD, TO WAIT

STUART HAMBLEN

Slowly, In A Western Style

WERE YOU THERE?

Spiritual
Arranged by Fred Bock

GOD GAVE THE SONG

WILLIAM J. and GLORIA GAITHER
& RONN HUFF
Arranged by Fred Bock

gradually building

A MIGHTY FORTRESS IS OUR GOD

Attributed to Martin Luther
Arranged by Fred Bock

Majestically, but not too slowly

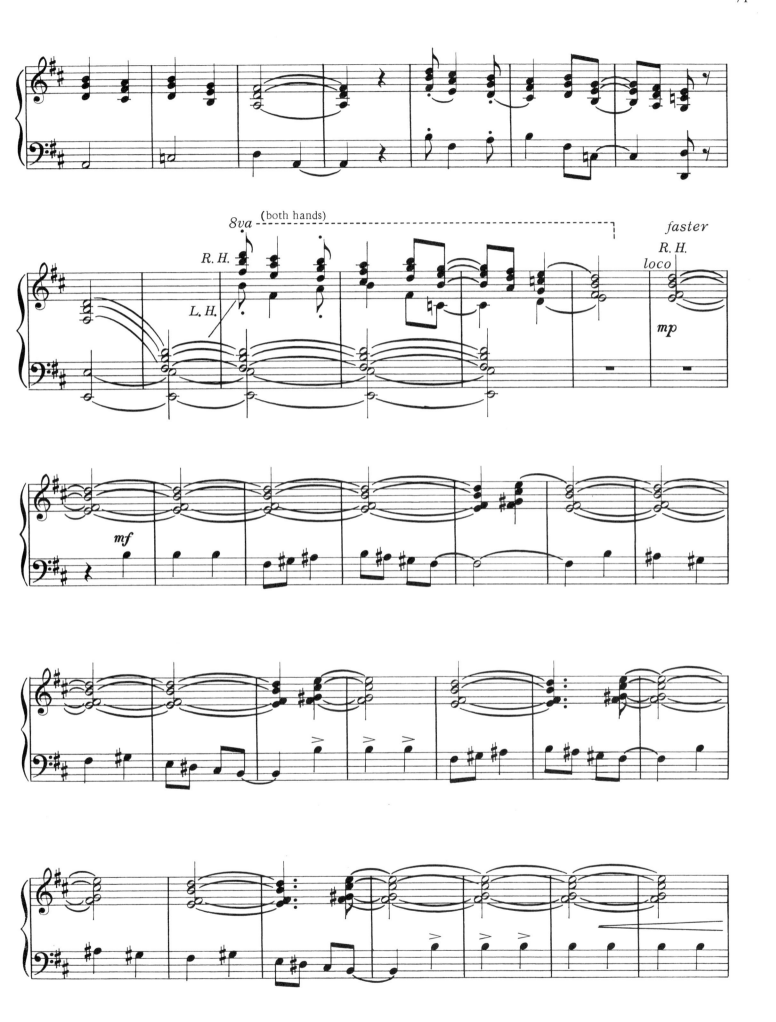

EVEN SO, LORD JESUS, COME

WILLIAM J. and GLORIA GAITHER
Arranged by Fred Bock

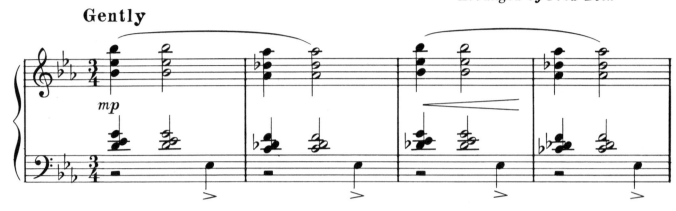

Good practice for crossing hands!

NOW I BELONG TO JESUS

NORMAN CLAYTON
Arranged by Fred Bock

78

MY FAITH LOOKS UP TO THEE

LOWELL MASON
Arranged by Fred Bock

Moderato

IVORY PALACES

HARRY BARACLOUGH
Arranged by Fred Bock

HOW BIG IS GOD?

STUART HAMBLEN

Moderato

A Little Brighter

In Tempo

* Play A and B♮ with side of thumb.

WHAT A FRIEND WE HAVE IN JESUS

CHARLES CONVERSE
Arranged by Fred Bock

Downstem notes should be held down to sustain.

TELL ALL THE WORLD ABOUT LOVE

RON *and* CAROL HARRIS
Arranged by Fred Bock

Bright shuffle tempo

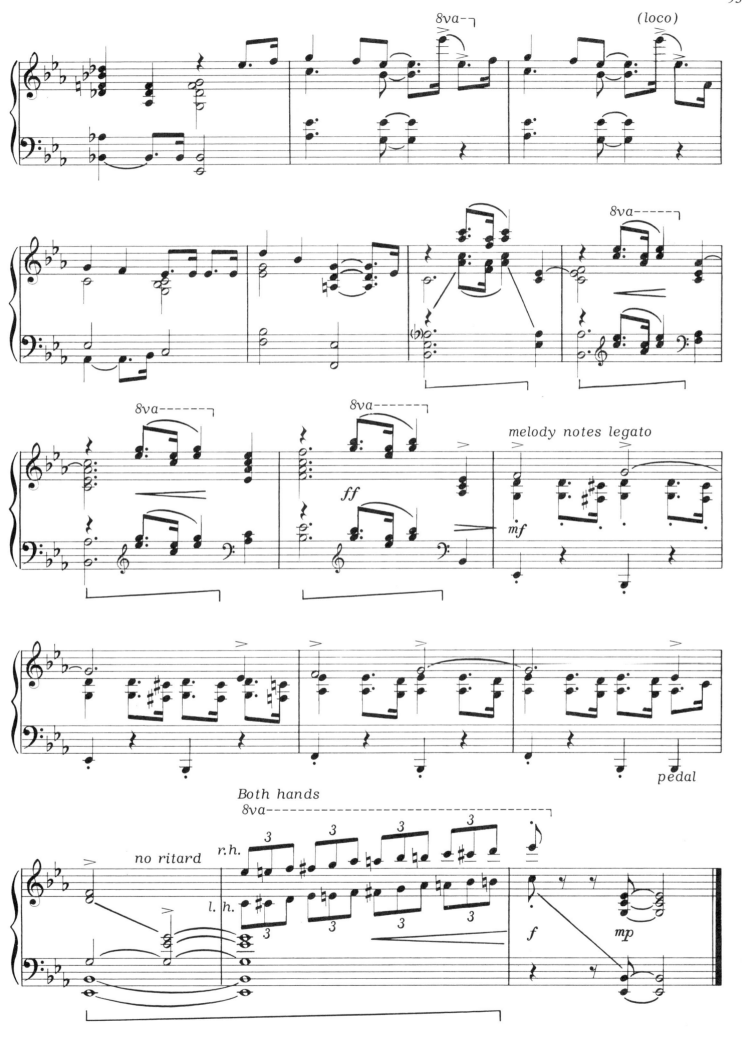

THERE'S SOMETHING ABOUT THAT NAME

Words and Music by
GLORIA and WILLIAM J. GAITHER
Arranged by Fred Bock

MANSION OVER THE HILLTOP

IRA STANPHILL
Arranged by Fred Bock

Warmly, not too slowly

Broaden (*accent melody notes*)

Mansion - 3

Mansion - 3

ROOM AT THE CROSS FOR YOU

IRA STANPHILL
Arranged by Fred Bock

Meditatively, with feeling

A little faster

REVIVE US AGAIN

JOHN HUSBAND
Arranged by Fred Bock

PRECIOUS LORD, TAKE MY HAND

TRADITIONAL SPIRITUAL
Arranged by Fred Bock

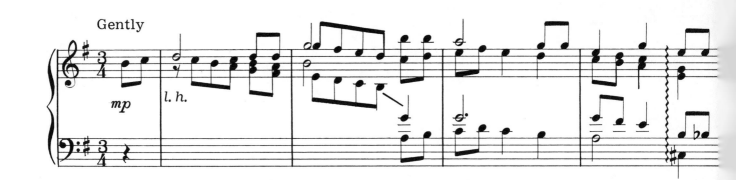

ONE SOLITARY LIFE

FRED BOCK
Arranged by Fred Bock

110

NARRATION *Spoken:*

1. Born in an obscure village, he was the child of a peasant woman. He
2. But when he was only thirty-three years old, the tide of public

(1) worked in a carpenter shop until he was thirty years old, an then for
(2) opinion turned against him, and his friends all rejected him. When he was

(1) three years he travelled around the country, stopping long enough to
(2) arrested very few wanted anything to do with him. After the trial he was

(1) talk and listen to people and help where he could. He never wrote a book
(2) executed by the State along with admitted thieves. Only because a generous

(1) he never had a hit record, he never went to college, he never ran for public off-
(2) friend offered his own cemetery plot was there any place to bury him. This all

(1) ice, he never had a family or owned a house. He never did any of the things
(2) happened nineteen centuries ago, and yet he is the leading figure of the human

(1) that usually accompany greatness. He had no credentials but himself.
(2) race and the ultimate example of love. Now it is no exaggeration to say that

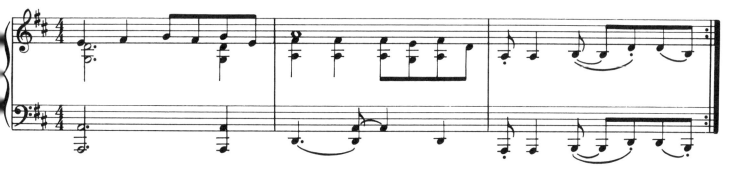

Brighter
All the armies that have ever marched, all the navies that have ever

112

set sail; All the rulers that have ever ruled, all the

kings that have ever reigned on this earth, all put together have not

affected the life of man on earth like this

One Solitary Life!

GENTLE SHEPHERD

Words and Music by
WILLIAM J. and **GLORIA GAITHER**
Arranged by Fred Bock

115

THE BOND OF LOVE

OTIS SKILLINGS
Arr. by Fred Bock

ALL FOR JESUS

ANONYMOUS
Arranged by Fred Bock

HE IS THE WAY

OTIS SKILLINGS
Arr. by Fred Bock

Bright, fast, and happy

123

124

SAFE AM I

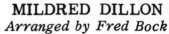

MILDRED DILLON
Arranged by Fred Bock

a little slower

warmly

Safe Am I - 2

HOW LONG HAS IT BEEN?

MOSIE LISTER
Arranged by Fred Bock

130

TO BE FREE

EDDIE SMITH
Arr. by Fred Bock

I BELIEVE IN MIRACLES

JOHN W. PETERSON
Arr. by Fred Bock

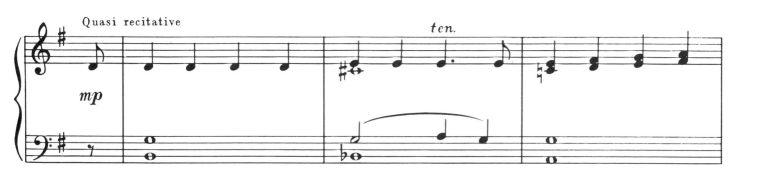

136

In a flowing style

mf

ten.

ten.

OPEN UP YOUR HEART AND LET
THE SUN SHINE IN

STUART HAMBLEN

Moderato

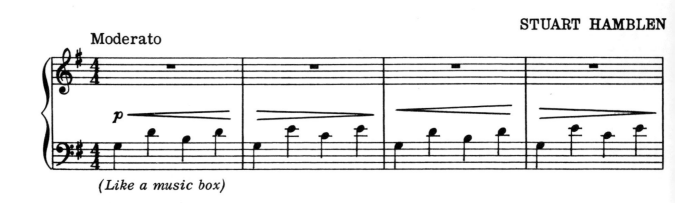

(Like a music box)

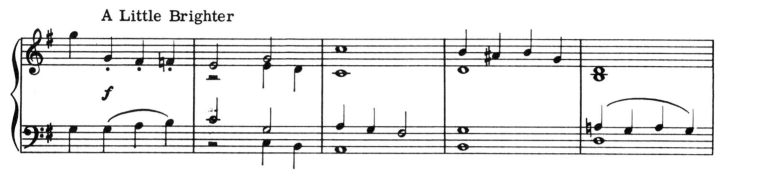

A Little Brighter

Still Brighter

140

Broaden

As In The Beginning

8va - - - - - - - - - - - - - - - - -

REDEEMING LOVE

WILLIAM J. and GLORIA GAITHER
Arranged by Fred Bock

I WILL SERVE THEE

WILLIAM J. and GLORIA GAITHER
Arranged by Fred Bock

Tenderly

THERE IS A BALM IN GILEAD

TRADITIONAL SPIRITUAL
Arranged by Fred Bock

Moderato

Brighter

as in the beginning

l.h.

SURELY GOODNESS AND MERCY

JOHN W. PETERSON
and ALFRED B. SMITH
Arranged by Fred Bock

In Western style

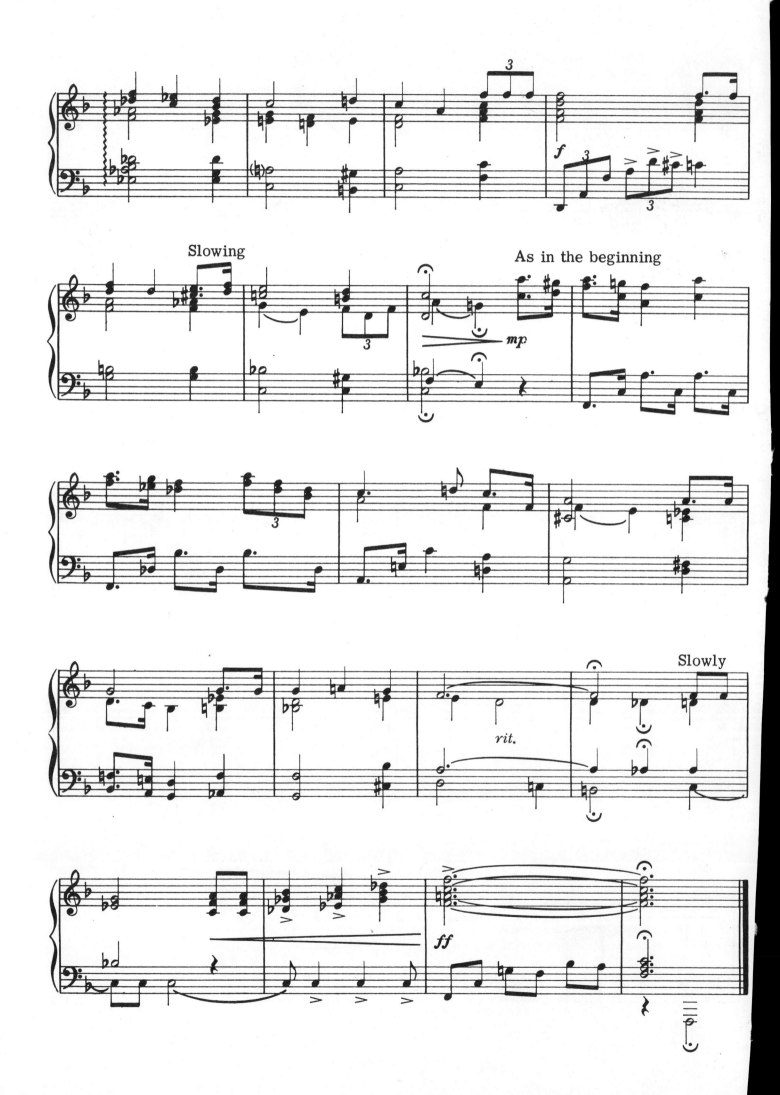